Digital Age Passive Income

Start your Location-Independent Journey Today!

Table Of Contents

Table Of Contents	II
Introduction	III
Chapter 1: What Is Passive Income?	1
Chapter 2: Self-Publishing	3
Chapter 3: Travel Blogging	8
Chapter 4: Affiliate Marketing	13
Chapter 5: Dropshipping	17
Chapter 6: Fulfillment By Amazon (Fba)	25
Chapter 7: Real Estate Investing	28
Chapter 8: Real Estate Investment Trusts	33
Chapter 9: Other Crowdfunding Platforms	38
Chapter 10: Other Passive Income Ideas	41
Conclusion	47

Introduction

I want to thank you and congratulate you for downloading the book Digital Age Passive Income: Start your Location-Independent Journey Today!

This book contains proven steps and strategies on how to become a truly successful entrepreneur and investor through the use of passive income streams. You can live the life you want, anywhere in the world, on your terms once you learn the key concepts in this book.

Here's an inescapable fact: You will need sources of income that work when you do not to get ahead and live the life you have always wanted. You can achieve this lifestyle starting with items and resources you already have.

If you do not develop your ability to create income sources that work twenty-four hours a day, seven days a week, you may find yourself stuck in a dead-end job, struggling to make ends meet while your employer gets rich from your labor. Partnering with the world's largest online retailer, making money in real estate, and being your own publisher are a few of the highlights in this book.

It is time for you to become an amazing entrepreneur with these passive income hacks, tips, and tricks. It is easy to find the right income sources for you that allow you to become your own boss, set your own hours, and live where and how you choose, on your own terms. This book helps you find a way to use your interests and even the items you already have in your own home, to get started. Whether you are looking to supplement your income, or are ready to live the passive income dream, the tips within these pages will make it easier for you. Once you learn these various options, from making money while traveling the world to watching your investments grow, you will never look at how you make money the same way again.

Chapter 1: What Is Passive Income?

For most of us these days, we earn the money we need to live by trading hours of our lives for a set amount of dollars. At the end of the week, we get our check, pay our bills, and the process starts over again. Week after week. Year after year.

The good news is that it does not have to be this way! Many people just like you and me have broken the cycle of living to work instead of working to live through the creation of passive income sources. In other words, they have set up ways to make money that do not depend on a set number of hours worked. And the best part is, they can do it from pretty much anywhere there is an internet connection.

Instead of getting paid for 40 (or more) hours of labor every week, these people travel, spend time with family, and just live life to the fullest where and how they choose, while their money works for them!

You can do this, too.

There are some important things to remember:

- These are not get-rich-quick schemes. Steady income streams take time to build, but can be well worth the effort.
- Passive income does not mean "no work" income. Some types of businesses require online engagement to attract and retain customers. Other types of income will require that you pay attention to changes in the market. This means you may not

be able to "set it and forget it" when it comes to your money!

- Passive income is not without some risk. This is especially important if you decide on investing, especially in real estate. Research is key, but well worth the effort.

- Depending on the type of passive income stream you choose, there may be up-front costs. Others require less money, but more initial effort.

Are you still interested? Great! Let's go.

Chapter 2: Self-Publishing

Writing a book and getting it published has never been easier. With e-books and print-on-demand technology, partnering with companies like Amazon and Barnes & Noble can help you get your book out to a waiting world, full of readers. Writing and producing a quality book that people will want to buy will require an investment of time and money, but after your book is finished and listed, it is available to buy (and earn you royalties) day and night to a world-wide marketplace.

Here are some key advantages:

Writing a book can help add to your other sources of income. When you are the author of a book, people regard you as an authority, and people will take you more seriously. This adds to your credibility, raising your profile and your value. Having print copies of your book with you allows you to sell on the spot to interested readers. Also, your book can also lead to paid speaking engagements, and more opportunities to gain new paying customers.

Let's say you want to be a travel blogger (we will discuss this more in Chapter 3). Being able to mention your book on your travel blog (and your blog in your book) can help channel the audience from one platform to the other. This increase in web traffic and sales numbers can pay off in other ways, too. We will see how shortly.

So How Do You Get Started?

First, find a topic you enjoy and know well. Do you like to cook? Write a cook book. Do you have a background in starting a business? That is information that people will pay for. Do you have specialized knowledge about a town's history? People are always interested in where they come from. Can you fix cars? People always need a guide to help them save money with auto repairs. Are people coming to you for investment advice? You can advise them to download your guide to answer their questions. Your finished book can help you with other passive income streams, so link the two if you can.

Second, Gather and Organize Your Thoughts

This does not have to be fancy or grammatical. If your notes make sense to you, your system works. Use lists, index cards, the message function on your phone, notebooks, specialized apps on your phone, anything, to start gathering the ideas that could make for a book people will want to buy. I say "could," because it does not have to be perfect at this stage. It just has to get started.

Do not be afraid to try different methods of note taking, too. What works for one person may be useless to another. What is important is making the time, even a few minutes, every day to work on your book. Persistence pays, so put your action steps in your calendar and your schedule.

Third, Start Writing!

At this point, do not worry about finding "the perfect word." Just get everything down. Worry about grammar and spelling later. The important thing at this stage is taking your ideas and getting them written. There are no mistakes at this point. Just write something every day, and before you know it, you will have a complete draft.

Next, Start Editing

This is the point where you start to look at how the book is organized. Does it make sense, or do you need to add/subtract/move sections? Is the spelling correct? How is the grammar? It is a good idea to get another person to help with this part. Even if you are a great writer, it can be hard to spot the most basic errors when you are reading something you have written. Remember, even Stephen King has editors helping him with his books!

It is important to know that when anyone, an editor or a general reader, makes a comment about your book, it is not about you personally! Listen to what is being said and move on. The editor wants the same thing you do: a book that is the best it can be. Even a great book can lose thousands in sales if it has typographical or grammatical errors, so good book editor is worth his or her weight in gold.

The Next Step Is Covering It Up!

Even though most people buy e-books, it is important to get a great cover for your book, as websites like Amazon are packed with books and other graphics, so it is important that your cover stands out in a good way.

If you are a graphic designer, great! You will be able to put together an eye-catching cover for your book. For the rest of us, paying for a book cover will be a very worthwhile expense. Fortunately, it does not have to cost a lot of money. A quick online search can help you find services to get you that just-right book cover. Like editing, a great book cover can help your sales, but a bad book cover can kill an otherwise terrific publication.

Promotion

We are almost done! When the book is nearly ready to be published, you want to start promoting it. The type of book you have written will point you to the best way to promote it.

Are you writing about things to do with children? Parenting groups need to know about your book. Is it about crafts and hobbies? Reach out to the local craft store and offer to give a talk or teach a class (and they may even agree to stock your book, too). Getting advanced copies to bloggers and book reviewers is important (sending PDF copies is fine for this). Building an audience on social media is key, especially if your reader is the general public. There are many books and websites on how to do this. Doing a little every day towards promotion will pay off in big dividends.

Finally, Get Published!

Your book is written and edited. It has a great cover, and people are looking to buy. It is time to get it out there, right? Not so fast! You have a few choices to make. Amazon has made it very easy to upload and sell your book. They give you options in their terms and conditions that can affect how you can sell your book, where you can sell it, and how much money you can make per sale. Read these terms and conditions carefully, as they can change at any time, and you may want to make some changes of your own. Remember to periodically review how your book is listed online. New options may become available.

Pricing is also important. "Charm pricing" refers to the way people culturally respond to the price of an item: Commonly, people will buy something at $1.99 rather than $2.00, for example. Different cultures have different charm prices, so it is wise to be aware of this. You may want to search online for books that are similar you yours. How are they priced? How are they selling? This can help guide you. It is better to get a lot of sales at $2.99 than very few at $5.99.

Other options for online book selling include publishing with other services like Apple, Smashwords, and Book Baby along with (or instead of) Amazon. There are also audio books, including Audible (which is owned by

Amazon). People love audio books to listen to in the car or while at the gym, so do not overlook this book format.

Regardless of who you choose to publish and sell your book with, you want to make sure it is formatted correctly, so when the reader opens the print or e-book, it looks and reads the way you want it to. Each service provides guides and support, and if you have an editor and/or graphic designer, they should be able to help you with this as well. Correct formatting is important, not only for the look of the finished book, but because if it is not done correctly, your book's publication could be delayed, and that can cost you sales, so it is worth it to get it right the first time!

The Takeaway. Writing a book of your own is not as hard as it seems, and can be profitable, especially when used with other passive income streams. The key is to find the right topic, work on it a little each day, and do not be afraid to bring in professional help to make your book the best it can be. Your ideas, and your bottom line deserve it!

Chapter 3: Travel Blogging

Who would not love to get paid to travel to exotic destinations? You can spend your springtime in Rome, head off to the Orient, and then travel South Pacific in winter. For some, this source of passive income is their reality. While it seems easy, there is lots of work involved, but for those who choose this lifestyle, it is well worth the effort.

Planning Ahead

Although it would be great to jump on a plane and start making money, most successful travel bloggers will tell you that a lot of planning is required before you even get your passport. As we have discussed, this is not a get-rich-quick scheme, so you do want to have money saved well before you start your travels. Exactly how much you should budget will depend on who you are, what your requirements will be, and where you will be going. For example, a 20-something backpacking through South America could live on much less per day than a couple with small children who want to blog from Hawaii. As with the other options for passive income, research and preparation is the key.

Another thing to consider is your market niche. What will set you apart from all the other travel blogs fighting for audience share? You have to know your market, see what others do that works, figure out how you can improve what does not, and decide what you can do differently to set yourself apart. Once you answer these questions, you have to persistently promote your brand, both on your website and via social media.

Flexibility

Think about the last vacation you took. Were there flight delays? Did someone in your party get sick or injured? Did you lose your luggage? Did you learn about a great little side-trip in your travels that you just could not explore?

These can cause inconveniences when you are away from home for a week or two, but can be absolutely catastrophic when travel is how you make your livelihood. Flexibility is the key. This includes your revenue streams. Changing market conditions demand that you have more than one income source, if not several, at one time. The good, and bad news, is that the options change constantly.

Having a tourism bureau pay for you to write about their beaches may be great, but it is generally not steady enough to depend on full time. Many bloggers also license photographs, post videos on YouTube, monetize their websites by selling ads using Google AdSense, among others, as well as affiliate marketing (see chapter 4).

Writing books about your travels, as well as how-to books about making the most of travel are invaluable and popular sources of passive income. There is more about writing your book in chapter 2. The key to all of these options is to make the most of your web traffic. You want to drive readers to your website, stay there, and spend their money with you.

Social Media

Social media is absolutely vital if you want to make a living as a travel blogger. Your ability to earn money, in large part, is based on attracting and engaging a large audience. Facebook, Pinterest, Twitter, Instagram, YouTube, and Snapchat are just a few of the ways people world-wide are connecting with content providers, but they all require careful planning, a firm grasp of who you are as a travel blogger, who it is you want to attract (note that "everyone" is not the answer), and knowing how to engage with your followers.

To get and keep your audience, you have to post often, if not several times per day, with photos and stories that people will want to see and share with friends. Not only does this demand your continued attention, there are the practical requirements of quality audio and video equipment, as well as at least some internet access are a must. Contingency plans if something breaks, gets stolen, or goes wrong are especially important. This goes back to planning and being flexible.

Your Blog

The key to this income stream is going to be your website and blog. It is where your audience will be able to find you while you are out globe-trotting. It should be able to handle a lot of traffic. It should be easy to find (an easy to remember domain name is vital here). It should also be simple to navigate both as a desktop page or when viewed on a mobile device. You also want to make sure that the webpage does not take too long to load, especially as you will have lots of graphics, photos, and video. You do not want to go through all the trouble of putting together great content, only to lose readers who will not come back because the website was slow, cluttered, or hard to navigate.

If you are tech savvy, you could do much of the design and maintenance yourself. If you are not, you may want to either get additional tech support as part of your site hosting fees, or have a dedicated webmaster. This is especially important if your travels take you to remote locations where internet access is not reliable. You do not want to come back from a few weeks in the back country to discover your website has been down the whole time! You also want to be sure the website is safe from hackers and viruses. Both can result in having your website blocked by anti-virus programs. Once a website gets the reputation of being a source for viruses, or malware it can be very hard to get traffic to come back to it.

Video/Podcasting

Another way to engage your audience while adding to your income stream is to have a video or podcasting channel. Popular channels on YouTube are easy to monetize through Google AdSense. You can also have a paid or free podcasting channel on Apple's iTunes, with links on your website. Video is a great way to get your audience involved, share exotic locations, and promote books, travel guides, public appearances, as well as partner sites. You could do this with the video app on your phone, but it pays to have proper audio and video equipment.

E-Mail Lists

While social media is very vital if you are using your blog as a passive income source, individual sites can become more or less important to you and your audience. Remember that access to your audience via Facebook, Instagram, and so on is controlled by the individual companies. They are trying to monetize their content, just like you are. What is free today can become a costly premium option tomorrow. An adjustment to algorithms can affect who sees what posts and when. The control you have in these cases is limited. You do, however own your email list, so it is very important that you encourage your audience to sign up and make your emails a priority.

There are many email options that are free or low-cost, easy to use, and will help you reduce the chance that your email is considered spam, which will affect your ability to get information out to your audience. Investing time researching and setting up your email host will pay you dividends in the future.

What can be included in a newsletter to your email list? You can include buy links to affiliates as well as to your books and other items on your online store, links to your blog, and YouTube channel. You should also include a short newsy post as well as some "exclusive" content. Previewing a popular feature from your YouTube channel or website to your email list is a great way to offer exclusivity without extra work.

Once the template for your newsletter is set up, it only takes minutes to send out an email to your audience, and most programs will provide data on opened emails, changes in your list, and other important information at no extra charge. You only need to send it out once a week to once a month, but it can pay big dividends to your bottom line.

The Takeaway. Travel blogging is not for everyone. There is a great deal of work and risk. However, if it is something you would want to do anyway, it is worth it to investigate this option. You want to take your time researching your options, save as much as you can before you start your travels, and work on a robust social media presence before you start heading out. Safe travels!

Chapter 4: Affiliate Marketing

Affiliate marketing can be a great way to add to your other passive income strategies. It is little more than buy links to partner sites that earn you money when the person who clicks the link purchases the product or service. It is a sales commission for something you are posting anyway to an audience you already have with little or no extra work.

An example would be your theoretical travel blog. You post about your stay in a tropical location and mention how well some light-weight rain gear performed. You add some pictures of you wearing it, and mention at the end of your post "you can get the same thing I'm wearing here," and you provide a link to the website. People click on the link, buy the jacket, and you get a percentage. Easy!

Pros

- This type of marketing is pretty seamless and easy to add on to your other marketing efforts.

- You do not have to stock any merchandise, nor do you have to worry about advertising, order fulfillment, or anything else.

- You do not have to design or manufacture the item.

Cons

- You have to research the item and the company before you add any links to your site. You have worked hard to build your audience, and if there are any issues with an item you recommend, it can damage your relationship with your customer base.

- You have to be selective. People respond to exclusivity. A few well-chosen affiliate links will get a better response than a hundred so-so ones. Again, pushing one affiliate after another on your audience will come off as spammy, and a turn-off.

- You have to be transparent. You want your audience to trust you. If you give them affiliate links or promote merchandise, destinations, and so on, without telling them that you are in an affiliate partnership, they can feel betrayed. A quick mention at the end is all it takes. Transparency is key.

- You need lots of traffic. Affiliate marketing is a numbers game. If a thousand people visit your website, one hundred may read a particular post. If a hundred people read your post, ten might click the affiliate link. If ten click the link, one may buy.

- You do not have the responsibilities of the vendor site, but you do not have any control over the vendor site. If there is an issue between your audience and the vendor, you can easily get caught in the middle.

So how can this work for you? You want to keep a few things in mind:

It is Not an Ad

If someone wants to buy ad space, then great. If you are including an affiliate link to your content, then do not make it read like advertising copy. You want to stick to the idea of "this works for me and it can work for you." You (hopefully) know your audience, so work with affiliates that will meet your audience's needs. You will not need to write ad copy. Solve a problem for someone already going to your website, and the product will sell itself. Spam your audience and they will not be your audience for long.

Try it Yourself

Go to another website that uses a prospective partner's links. Click through. What happens? Are you getting hit with pop-up ads? Are you getting spammed? Is your anti-virus software warning you about malware and pop-ups? What is the website like? If it is annoying to you, it will annoy your audience. You do not want that.

Do Not Flop Around

You want to pick a few affiliates, present them well, and give things time. You want to track what works and what does not, and especially while you are in the testing phase (and you should always be testing something), you want to keep the variables down to a minimum. Know what you are looking for and see where you can do better.

Affiliate marketing should be used to add to the other revenue streams you already have in place. You want to be very clear in your own mind what it is that you want to do, who you want to connect with, and how you can turn this connection into a source of income that is not dependent on trading an hour worked for a set dollar amount. This takes patience, focus, and self-discipline. When it comes to affiliate marketing, the value you are selling to the partner site, what you are really getting paid for, is access to your audience. It is very important that you make the growth and well-being of your client base a priority.

The Takeaway. You would not be able to use this method to its fullest all by itself. Used as part of a bigger passive income strategy, however, it could do very good things to your bottom line. The important things to remember is to be choosy, remember that your most important asset is the visitor to your web page, and for this method to be effective, you need to get as many people to the links as often as possible.

Chapter 5: Dropshipping

While creating a client base to sell books or support you while you travel the globe may be great, it may not be the right fit for you. What else can you to generate passive income? One option is to set up a virtual storefront, either on Shopify, Amazon, or any number of other websites without the hassle of maintaining inventory. This is commonly called "dropshipping."

How this works is that an online store is created. As products are ordered, they are shipped directly from the factory or a wholesaler to the customer.

Benefits

- Ease of startup. You do not have to purchase or store any inventory. You can also run your store from virtually anywhere, as long as you have internet access. This makes for a very low initial investment that can be run anywhere.

- Low Overhead Costs. You are not responsible for manufacturing or storing any of your product line. You also do not have to worry about shipping or returns. This means you can run a thriving business on a laptop without a lot of startup costs.

- Flexibility. Because you do not have to create, store, or ship your goods, you are free to change up your offerings at any time. You can also expand your business without too much effort. As long as you can communicate with your suppliers, promote your online store, and maintain good customer service, there is no limit to your growth.

Minuses

- Supplier issues. As with the affiliate market, you are free from the issues of supply, but you have little, if any, control over issues that come up. If a customer pays you for an item and there is a problem with it, you still have the responsibility of making it right, even if the issue was not due to anything you did. This includes, but is not limited to shipping delays, either due to a requested item being unavailable or because of a problem with the postal or delivery service, items missing or received broken, or the customer getting the wrong color, size or item.

- Problems can also arise when you have more than one supplier for your items. Coordinating the shipping can be a problem that may need to be handled one order at a time, as opposed to an automated process. This can slow down the shipping process and require dedicated employees, and extra shipping costs, which will drive up your expenses.

How Dropshipping Works

Items for sale are listed on the website and the customer places an order either with a sales agent or online. The customer's payment is taken, and the order is placed with the wholesaler or manufacture. The third party then charges the retailer. The order is then shipped directly to the customer who placed the original order.

The retailer is notified of the shipment and contacts the customer. The shipping materials all have the retailer's name and information, so the customer is not aware of the third party. The profit the retailer makes is the difference between what was collected by the customer and charged by the third party.

Wholesaler Fine Print

Once your vendors are in place, it can be very smooth, as we can see. As always, getting set up requires due diligence and research, as scams and pitfalls are out there.

Legitimate wholesalers will only work with other businesses, not individuals. Before listing their items on your store website, wholesalers will require that you set up an account with them and provide documentation that you are in fact a registered business.

Also, you should not be getting charged any "membership fees." There are, however, some fees that above-board wholesalers will charge, including transaction fees (usually only a few dollars per order), and minimum order requirements. Honest businesses will disclose all fees and conditions beforehand. Always read the fine print and ask questions.

Finding Your Suppliers

Once you decide what items you want to offer, the next step is finding wholesalers to work with. As they do not do business with the public, you have to work a little harder to find these suppliers.

- Trade Shows. Trade Shows are great ways to network with suppliers and find potential vendors. There is an investment of time and money involved, but if you have a good idea of what you want to offer, trade shows allow you to develop your list of wholesalers over the course of a day or two. Sales reps are generally working the vendor booths at trade shows, and often can offer show specials, so it can be worth your while to try and attend at least one show, if it is feasible.

- Supplier Directories. These are lists of wholesalers in a given industry. Some have to be purchased, but others are free from their respective associations. They generally include the business name and contact information, and very often web site addresses.

- Manufactures. Some manufactures handle their own wholesale distribution. Some manufactures do not. It is always worthwhile to contact the companies who make the products you are interested in selling. If they do not ship to end customers, they can often refer you to the wholesalers they work with.

Getting Set Up

As was mentioned earlier, you need to be a retail business to work with a wholesaler. This means registering as a business with your state or local government. You also want to present yourself professionally. The more prepared you are when talking to potential vendors, the better off you will be. Having specific information about what you are looking for will get you better results from wholesalers.

Finding Great Suppliers

The wholesaler you will be working with can make or break your business, so it is worth it to make sure the company you keep will not let you down. Some things you want to look for include:

- Knowledgeable sales staff. Can your sales rep answer your questions? What does he or she know about the industry? Does this person keep you in the loop about new products or issues?

- Customer Service. If a problem comes up, who can you contact to get it resolved? The wholesaler's client services department are, for all intents and purposes, your company's client services department, too. Can they address all issues quickly?

- Communication. You cannot go down to the warehouse to see how things are going. Is there any way you can quickly find out what the wholesaler has in stock and for how much? If things are on back order, how long will they be unavailable? How do you they communicate with you regarding delays?

- Logistics. Where are their items shipping from? Is it from a central hub, or are there fulfillment centers in several locations? The quicker your customer can get the order, the better. If the customer has to wait even an extra day, it will cause you to lose business and money.

Finding Your Customer Base

Having to constantly locate new clients can take a lot of time, effort, and advertising dollars. While you want to grow your list of clients all the time, you also want to develop a solid core of repeat buyers. They include:

- Collectors. Depending on your market, collectors can boost your bottom line. You only need to go to a fan convention once to see collectors in action. They will not get just one of anything. They want the whole set in every color, and they will pay a premium to complete their collections. If you can tap into a robust fan base (think Harry Potter or Star Wars), you can achieve a steady stream of orders.

- Returning Buyers. If your business deals in items that need to be reordered, keeping the customer satisfied and making automated reorders easy can help you grow your business. Examples of items in this category include health and beauty supplies, water filters, and specialty pet foods.

- Hobbyists. Like collectors, hobbyists want what they want and will pay a premium for it. If you can find a niche market that you can serve on a regular basis, it can do great things for your bottom line.

Pricing

As was noted before, your profit is what the customer pays, minus what you pay the wholesaler (less your expenses). When you set your prices, you want to be careful. Depending on the items and your customer, they may want to talk to an actual person before handing over their credit card information. Depending on your agreement with your wholesaler, there may be limits on how low or high you can set pricing. Again, read the fine print and know your market.

Getting Started

In addition to setting up your business legally, finding your market niche, and locating wholesalers, there are a few other things you need to keep in mind:

- This is not a get-rich-quick scheme. It will take effort, especially if you are still working at a day job while the business is getting established. Industry averages suggest that it takes approximately twelve to eighteen months for an online shopping site to become profitable enough to allow you to leave your 40 hour a week job.

- It can be worth it. After the initial setup, time requirements are less, allowing the business to run and grow while you are still at the full-time position.

- The business can become a material asset. If you choose, the business can be sold. This is not a bad outcome for something that was built during "spare" time from a laptop computer.

Dropshipping on Merchant Websites

As part of creating an online storefront, one generally has to create an online store for potential customers to shop on. There are alternatives, namely places like Shopify, eBay, and Amazon.

The advantages include millions of potential customers. There is no worry about Google rankings or SEO, or building a website. This can save you a great deal of time. This also allows you to get started sooner, and, hopefully, become profitable more quickly.

These are huge advantages, but the downside is important to consider, too: They include listing and commission fees, having to constantly re-list items (especially on eBay), the inability to customize your web page, the collection of your sales data (especially on Amazon), and the inability to grow your own client base.

Generally, you have more control when you have your own website, but it requires the investment of time and money to set up, optimize for Google search ranking, and it tends to be more complex. One method is to list some items on shopping sites as you get your store website up and running. Explore your options carefully.

The Takeaway. Dropshipping can be a great way to open up your own internet-based business without the heavy investment in stock. This type of business does require work, especially in the early stages. Careful research and not skipping steps is the key to success.

Chapter 6: Fulfillment by Amazon (FBA)

As was mentioned in Chapter 5, you can dropship orders made on Amazon, but you also have to option of having Amazon fulfill your orders directly, too.

How it works is that you set up an account on Amazon. You then list the items you wish to sell on the retail website. You ship the items to Amazon's warehouse facilities. Once it has entered their inventory, it goes live on the website and it is available to order.

The advantages are many:

- Millions of potential customers.

- There is no worry about Google rankings or SEO

- You do not have to build a website

- It can save you a great deal of time. This allows you to get started sooner, and, hopefully, become profitable much more quickly.

- There are no minimums. If you have a new item in its original packaging, you could list it and send it to Amazon to be included on their website.

- If you have an account with a wholesaler, you could have them send the entire shipment to Amazon directly, as long as the items are already packaged for individual sale.

- Shipping, payments, and customer service are handled by Amazon.

- As an FBA merchant, your products are eligible for free shipping to Prime members, including Sunday delivery at no extra charge. This can be a very powerful marketing tool.

- Potential customers will trust a name they know (Amazon), already have their credit card information on file with them, and will be more likely to spend money on your products than they would if they came directly to your website.

- Because Amazon takes the payment from the customer, you are much less likely to have to deal with fraudulent payments then you would if you had your own storefront.

There are disadvantages as well:

- They include monthly listing and commission fees. Depending on the option, it can be $.99 per item or $39.99 per month at the time this book was written. Picking, weight, and storage fees also apply.

- The inability to customize your web page.

- The collection of your sales data.

- The inability to grow your own client base.

As you can see, if you have access to merchandise that will move fairly quickly and you are willing to trade flexibility and a part of your profitability to have a retailing giant deal with shipping and payment collection, this may not be a bad option. This could also be worthwhile as part of other income sources, or to move small lots of merchandise that otherwise would not be a good fit as part of a larger retail plan.

As always, be prepared to research your options, read the fine print, and put in the time and effort needed for results.

The Takeaway: Amazon can be a great partner in your internet-based business. You have to remember that if you choose to do business with them, it will be on their terms. However, for many people, the trade-off can be well worth it.

Chapter 7: Real Estate Investing

Investing in real estate, when done properly, has long been considered an excellent opportunity for the shrewd investor.

Reasons why real estate is a good investment:

- Cash flow: Once you have a tenant, you have a steady income flow. Often times, the cash from rental properties can outperform the stock market.

- Leveraging assets. Real estate can be used to back loans, allowing the investor to purchase more property, which can then be rented or leased out, increasing cash flow.

- Better debt. Because loans can be backed by real assets, it is possible to negotiate better loan terms, saving you money.

- Hedge against inflation. As the value of the dollar rises and falls, real estate can help to stabilize an investment portfolio.

- It is a physical asset. The land, and buildings, as well as any income produced are considered hard assets, and therefore a stable asset.

- Tax benefits. Mortgage interest and the deferment of taxable gains are only a few of the advantages of owning property. Always see your tax adviser for more details.

- Asset Appreciation. Property historically increases in value in the face of inflation, especially as rents increase, improving cash flow.

Typical sources of investment properties include:

- Market listings.
- Real estate agents and Real estate brokers.
- Banks.
- Government agencies.
- Estate sales, foreclosures, and other public auctions.
- Private sales by the property owner.
- Real estate wholesalers and investors ("flipping").

Everyone has heard of the guy who put no money down and made thousands flipping houses. In today's market, the smarter investment involves time, careful research, due diligence, and the acquisition of "boring" rental properties with stable, long-term tenants.

Once you have found some property that may be suitable for investment, research is always needed. Before you invest any money into the property, you have to know the condition of the land and any buildings, as well as what the status of the property is, including title history. If that checks all out, negotiations with the owner can begin. Once terms are reached, an agreement is signed, and the property is said to be "under contract." It pays to have an attorney who specializes in real estate, as local laws can be confusing, and it can be very expensive to make any errors during the transaction.

Generally, mortgages are taken out to pay for the property. The amount taken out is calculated into the measure of risk the investor is being exposed to as part of the transaction. This will affect the return on investment (ROI). If the property is in very poor condition (as can happen with foreclosed or "flipped" properties), additional financing, including "hard money loans" may be needed to complete the transaction. Hard money loans tend to have much higher interest rates than traditional mortgages, due to increased risk.

It can take a while for an investment property to become profitable. Especially if it is in poor condition and not "move-in ready," and expenses can mount quickly. It is important for the investor to manage cash flow carefully, so negative cash flow periods can be offset by positive cash flow.

In addition to selling properties, other sources of income include:

- Net Operating income (NOI). This includes rents and other income, minus expenses, including taxes, maintenance, and other expenses, not including debt.

- Equity. The worth of the property less debt. As you pay off your mortgage, the equity in the property increases.

- Tax Shelter Offsets. This is basically anything that reduces the tax burden of the property. It includes depreciation and tax credits.

- Capital Appreciation. This reflects the increase of the value of the property over time. If you are thinking of buying a property with the idea of profiting from an anticipated increase of the value, it is considered less of an investment and more of land speculation. This is very risky and not recommended as part of a long-term investment strategy

Risk Management

Risk is always going to be a part of real estate investments. There are things you can do to lessen the risk. As always, careful research and consulting with legal counsel is always recommended.

- Tax planning. Begin with the end in mind. Planning to keep a property long-term versus short-term will require different strategies. Getting a tax advisor involved early in the process is a good idea.

- Personal Injury, Fire, flood. Always carry the appropriate insurance policies.

- Property maintenance. Bring in plumbers, electricians, and so on, as needed to maintain the property. Routine maintenance will save money in the long run.

- Decline in the Market. Plan on declines in the market and invest conservatively as appropriate.

- Underestimation of Risk. Research the market and property carefully. Ensure that the property can maintain positive cash flow in the face of temporary down-turns.

- Destruction of the Property by Tenants. Make use of experienced property managers and screen tenants carefully.

- Downturns in the Economy. Make use of long-term leases for tenants and watch costs.

- Income Shortfall. Keep a cash reserve.

- Over-payment of Property. Research the market and property, using more than one source of information if possible.

- Building Issues. Have the property fully inspected by an independent inspector prior to purchase. Maintain the property on a regular schedule.

- Environmental Issues. Have the property inspected for lead pain, soil contamination, and so on.

- Fraud. Carefully inspect the property, including a land survey, and research the title and ownership. Title insurance is also helpful.

Distressed Assets

One source of investment properties is through foreclosure auctions for the sale of distressed assets. The properties are generally vacant, and can be had for little more than what is owed to the lender. As always, caution and due diligence is warranted.

The Takeaway: Investing in real estate is a time-tested method of earning money through passive income. While it can be exciting to flip distressed properties like we see on TV, moving carefully, doing research, and acquiring "boring" properties with steady rental income are good ways to mediate risk and maximize positive cash flow.

Chapter 8: Real Estate Investment Trusts

Real Estate Investment Trusts (REITs) are a way for investors to enter the real estate market with less risk. They are considered an easy way to invest in real estate. REIT index mutual funds invest in many different kinds of real estate, spreading risk. The value of these investments are contingent on interest rates and the stock market, as opposed to local property value.

An important trend is the use of online platforms like RealityShares, Peer Street, and Fundrise.

RealtyShares. This is an online investment platform that facilitates real estate investment by acting as a one-stop shop for investors and borrowers. The focus is on smaller properties (usually single-family dwellings). In 2014 alone, RealtyShares did over $300 million in investments in seventeen different states. RealtyShares offers the option of investing in groups of properties, like a traditional REIT, or in a single property individually.

Investment opportunities are vetted by RealtyShares, and approved properties are listed on the site. Information listed includes legal documentation and risk factors associated with the property. Investors have the option of investing in a percentage of the property, up to 100%. The site also tracks earnings, and provides tax information for the investor. Options also include funding investments or loans on an individual property. Investors receive distributions quarterly as a direct deposit.

Benefits of investing through RealtyShares includes the flexibility to accumulate a portfolio of real estate investments, as opposed to being limited to a few properties. Clients can pick from a number of deals, including private equity positions or the funding of loans. Because of this, clients can take advantage of investment opportunities that had once only been an option of very large investors. Investors can diversify their investments as much or as little as they like, including types of properties, manner of investment, and even geographical location.

While the individual investor should do some research, RealtyShares vets each opportunity, including a background check of the principals, a review of the property inspection and title reports, and any other important information. Unlike other forms of real estate management, the day to day management of the properties is not the responsibility of the client.

At the time of publication, there are no registration fees to begin investing with RealtyShares. There is a 1% annual fee to manage equity investments. There may be some charges associated with other investment expenses. Debt investments are subject to a service fee applied the interest rate charged to the borrower. Registration is limited to accredited investors.

Fundrise. This is a service that allows the individual investor the ability to invest in commercial real estate via a crowdsourcing platform. The intent of Fundrise is to give access to larger real estate deals by way of a transparent online marketplace.

Fundrise is similar to other crowdsourcing platforms, like Lending Club and Prosper, but is focused on real estate investments. One of the aims of Fundrise is to provide an alternative for builders looking for short-term financing.

A good amount of projects available for investment on Fundrise do not require that the investor be accredited.

Annual fees range from 0.3-0.5% (Outstanding in this day and age) and distributions are made quarterly. After a 30 day cooling off period post-registration, the client buys in to investments through the purchase of $1,000.00 notes. A diverse portfolio may require the purchase of several of these notes. Each offer is given a risk rating, allowing the investor to participate in offers that match his or her investment comfort zone. There is no requirement to invest, and there is an IRA investment option.

While Fundrise does research each opportunity, investment always carries risk. Unless you go through the process yourself, assets are not liquid until the note matures, is defaulted upon, or if the debtor pre-pays the note. As always, investor beware.

Advantages to investing with Fundrise includes hands-off investing, as opposed to having to be involved in the day-to-day operation of the property. With the initial buy-in at $1,000.00, investors can start small in an investment sector that can be very expensive to get in to. Fees are also small, and are deducted from your returns.

PeerStreet. This crowdfunding service provides real estate loans by matching investors with borrowers. The aim of PeerStreet is to open real estate investment opportunities to lenders who may not otherwise be able to invest. Risk is minimized through the structure of the loans, as well as having all loans backed by hard assets. Unlike REITs, the investor can direct his or her investment. In a traditional REIT, the investment makes up a percentage of an individual loan.

Through PeerStreet, investors can help fund real estate loans, either in part or in their entirety. Generally, PeerStreet loans are first liens that are secured by the property. The loans are short-term, ranging from six to twenty-four months. There are a wide range of loan opportunities, with different property types, projects, and locations to choose from.

PeerStreet's team of real estate experts carefully vet out each new loan application, research loan originators, including financial statements, licensing, background checks, and so on. Of course, individual investors should always practice due diligence.

With PeerStreet, investors are able to choose where their money goes, as well as set up parameters for automated investing, adding the loans to the investors' portfolios automatically. Investors are also given information on loan originators, so they can be researched independently. Self-directed IRA accounts are also available.

Investor's funds are insured up to $250,000.00 per investor via and Investor's Trust Account. Loan defaults are referred to a dedicated team experienced in real estate law to protect investor assets.

The minimum deposit to open an account is $1,000.00 and fees range from 0.25-1.00% of each loan.

Advantages include stability of return, as investments are made in the form of loans only, diversification of investment options, limited interest rate risk, and a low minimum deposit.

Disadvantages include accredited investor requirements, the risk inherent in real estate loans, and non-liquid assets. As always, due-diligence is a must.

Although the bar to investment is a bit lower for PeerStreet than it is for other crowdfunding platforms, this option may not be for everyone. Because of the unorthodox nature of the loan offerings on PeerStreet, investors should be experienced in the real estate market, especially real estate loans and lending, so they may be prepared for the risks that this inherent in this type of investment. Investors prepared to take on high-risk in the real estate market would be interested in what PeerStreet has to offer.

The Takeaway. Overall, if you are looking to get into the real estate market, but you are not interested in the day-to-day management of an investment property, platforms like Fundrise, RealtyShares and PeerStreet can be a good way to help diversify your portfolio and earn passive income. If you do chose to put your money into one of these platforms, you should be prepared to take on moderately risky investments with options multiple to liquidate your investment assets. Because you would need to be an accredited investor (Fundrise being the exception), which would require a net worth of over $1 million ($200,000.00 with PeerStreet), this would not be an option for everyone, but could be a very good investment for the right person.

Chapter 9: Other Crowdfunding Platforms

If you are interested in crowdfunding, but not the risk associated with the real estate market, there are other options. Platforms like NextSeed and Lending Club offer investors the chance to help source not just real estate, but new businesses, and even personal loans.

Prior to these platforms, the only way for small investors to get involved with startups were websites like Indiegogo and Kickstarter. Now, non-accredited investors have other options. With NextSeed, businesses looking for funding must provide detailed plans for the funds, including business plans and financials. As the platform is designed with the new investor in mind, rules are in place to reduce risk, including an escrow account to return funds to investors if the project is not fully funded. Despite that, there is still inherent risk in any type of investment. Even with full funding, the vast majority of startups fail.

As the lines blur between donations and investment, sites like Kickstarter and Indiegogo have included stronger rules for applicants. Despite this, returns are still relatively small. The principals behind platforms are still optimistic that that this type of grass-roots investment can develop into a new wave of venture capitalism, but time will tell.

One does need to be careful, however. With platforms like Lending Club, investors have the option of backing loans to individuals. The money can be used for personal debt, among other reasons. Unlike real estate, this debt is unsecured, and far riskier. Although the borrower's risk rating is disclosed (as it is for Lending Club, for example), there is always the risk for default, with limited recourse to recover funds. In the case of unsecured personal loans, a default means that the investor not only loses interest that would have been made on the loan, but the original investment as well.

Lending Club does work to limit risk by setting a high bar for borrowers, with a minimum FICO score of 706 and no history of late payments for twelve months prior to application. Generally, the larger and more diverse the portfolio, the less an individual default will affect the lender's cash flow. Lending Club also provides tools to help investors manage risk and diversify their holdings. Generally, however, you are better off as a borrower than a lender

This risk-aversion is causing potential investors to consider options other than online lenders. Equity investment has dropped off sharply when you compare the first half 2016 to the last two quarters of 2015. In an effort to prop up falling loan volume, some lenders have lowered their loaning standards. This has resulted in an increase in defaults and late payments, which could drive away investment even further.

Other issues that would affect crowdfunding include:

- The reluctance of Americans to invest. This is an issue because if crowdfunding is to stabilize and become more of an attractive alternative for those seeking passive income, cash flow will have to increase. Unfortunately, most Americans do not have funds available to save for retirement, much less invest in crowdfunding platforms that are risky to begin with.

- Peer-to-Peer lending is a do-it-yourself option. Most Americans are unwilling or unable to manage the investments they do have. Unfortunately, platforms such as Lending Club require the investor to manage the account and make sure there is sufficient diversification to reduce risk. On top of that, there are risk grades to review, as well as hundreds of loans that are potential investments.

- Peer-to-Peer lending is not available everywhere. This makes it difficult for investment. Regulations are changing, but until that happens, growth will be slow.

- Minimum investment requirements. If people do not have enough to save for retirement, they are not likely to part with $1,000.00 to $2,000.00 they cannot spare for a confusing investment that may well cause them to lose money. And even if they do, that $1,000.00 to $2,000.00 will not be enough to get a diversified portfolio.

The Takeaway. While peer-to-peer funding has potential to become more of a driving force in the venture capital community, because of the risks involved, current regulations, and limited funds of risk-adverse investors, investors may want to tread very carefully, and only after a great deal of research and due-diligence.

Chapter 10: Other Passive Income Ideas

1. Sell Your Text Books and Electronics. Do you have text books, novels, or other books at home that are in good condition, but of no use to you anymore? Amazon gives shoppers the option of buying used books on their website. Gather up your old books, cell phones, DVDs, CDs, and electronics, search your items on the Amazon Trade-In Store and trade in your old items for Amazon gift cards, which are good for anything on the website. Shipping to Amazon is free, and you receive your credit within days of being received.

2. Flea Markets. If you do not want to go the Amazon route, flea markets are a great way to declutter your home and fatten your wallet. If you have unique items, such as antiques and other collectables, it can pay to locate a specialty flea market that attracts collectors who will pay more.

3. Investments. If you are not familiar with investing, getting a financial advisor who can guide you to investment options that work for your budget and comfort level is a time-tested way to put your money to work for you.

4. Selling on Etsy. Do you draw? Are you great with DIY projects? Do you knit, crochet, or quilt? You can create downloadable files and sell them on Etsy. There is no shipping involved, and PDF files of instructions and diagrams can be made in seconds and will be available twenty-four hours a day, seven days a week.

5. Taking Surveys. You can get paid for participating in surveys and focus groups. In addition, you could

get free products to try. You may not be able to retire on this income, but it could add up to hundreds of dollars per month for talking about items you would use daily anyway.

6. Credit Card/Cash Back Rewards. You buy gas and groceries anyway, why not get money back when you do? You can easily find cash back offers for credit or debit cards. A good place to start is the bank you currently do business with. Offerings from banks and other financial providers can be found online or in your mail box.

7. Airline Miles Programs. If you travel, you probably have an airline rewards card in your wallet. Many times, they have corporate partners that will help you earn travel rewards when you use their services as well. Make sure to give your rewards number so you do not miss out on reward points.

8. Certificates of Deposit. If you do not like risk, but do like money, investing in certificates of deposit may be a good option. Generally, online banks and credit unions can offer better rates, so it pays to shop around. The down side is that it can be hard to get at your money before the CD matures, but by investing in several certificates over time, you can eventually have interest income available on a regular basis.

9. Selling Items on eBay. Even if you have tried to sell items at a specialty flea market, sometimes you get a very unique item. By posting it on eBay, you can reach a much wider pool of interested buyers. There are several listing options, including "buy it now," which will let a buyer pay a set price to stop an auction. There are fees involved, but this is a

popular way to get unusual items to a wide audience.

10. Running an Auction Service. Sometimes, people want to sell items on eBay, but do not want to go through the hassles of setting up an account, putting together a listing, and all the other steps that make up the process. You could provide that service for them, in exchange for a percentage of the sale price and/or listing fee.

11. Licensing Photos. You do not have to be a professional photographer to license your original photos. All you have to do is submit them to websites that license stock photographs and you get a fee every time you license a photo.

12. Licensing Music. You can license your original music, too. Companies are always looking for music for use on videos, in places of business, and in movies or theater productions. Online services will list your composition and pay you for licensing it.

13. Online Classes. You can upload videos to online learning websites and get a fee when someone accesses it. What kind of courses can you teach? Pretty much anything: home repairs, tips and tricks for iPhones or Android devices, and many other skills can be taught online. Depending on what service you use, you can also upload handouts, diagrams, or other information, which can add value to your class and improve your bottom line.

14. Posting on YouTube. By linking your YouTube account to Google's AdSense, you can monetize your videos. Google will automatically link in ads and pay you every time they are viewed. The great part is that your videos can be about pretty much

anything. People cannot get enough of cute animals, crazy stunts, or even watching people unbox electronics. Anything you can post that will get people to your channel can make you money.

15. Create an App. If you own any kind of smart phone, you have used at least one app. Short for "application," they are the programs on your phone that let you play games, check your bank balance, and send messages, among a hundred other things. If you have ever told yourself "I wish they had an app that..." you are probably not alone. You can either create your own, or hire a programmer. Once it is listed in the Google Play store or the iTunes app store, you get a fee for every purchase. You can also create a "free" version of the app that comes with ads, and get revenue from advertising.

16. Storage Rental. Do you own a large piece of property? You could lease space to people looking to store large pieces of equipment. If you have a warehouse or other suitable building, you can also lease out storage units. This is a similar idea to leasing residential or office space, but is usually much cheaper to set up and maintain.

17. Airbnb. Do you have a spare room or is your house stilling empty from time to time? Listing it on Airbnb may be an answer. This service has been around for years, matching travelers with accommodation that is less expensive than traditional hotels. Especially if you are located near popular attractions or in a major city and can charge a premium, this can be a great way to make money.

18. Design T-Shirts and Mugs. Companies like Café Press and Society6 can take your original designs

and photos and turn them into t-shirts, phone covers, wall hangings, computer skins, and much more. It is all print-on-demand, so there is no cash outlay, need to purchase or store stock.

19. Network Marketing. If you have ever gone to a Pampered Chef party or ordered Avon products, you have experienced network marketing in action. You have the advantage of nationwide advertising and brand recognition, while setting your own hours. Through referrals, you can start earning a percentage of sales from people you sign up to sell items themselves.

20. Shopping Guide. This is a variation on the affiliate marketing plan we discussed in Chapter 4. Here, you compare two or more items and provide affiliate links. As a bonus, manufactures will often send free samples for you to try and talk about online.

21. Rent Tools. Do you have heavy equipment, automotive repair, or specialty tools? Unless you use them on a very regular basis, you can make good money renting them out. Even if it is not a very expensive item, people will be willing to rent a tool to complete a job, rather than buy it outright and have to store it.

22. Compile Public Information. While you may want to get some help with the data entry, you can compile, publish, and sell information that is in the public domain. Examples of this include listings of personal injury attorneys in Newark, New Jersey. People would be paying you, rather than spending their time searching for more than what is on the first page of a Google search.

23. Become a Silent Partner. You want to be very very careful here, but if you have extra money, but limited time or expertise, you can become a silent partner in a business. This does take research, and terms must be worked out ahead of time, especially when working with family or friends, but done correctly, this can be a great way to make money on a steady basis while the partner with the experience does the work.

24. Repackage Your Content. Do you have popular articles and posts on your blog? You can organize this information, put it in to one publication, and sell it on your website and/or Amazon. While the original information is available, people will pay for the convenience of having everything in one place that they can read on their electronic device.

25. Create a Paywall for Premium Content. Say you have a popular website with a ton of great information. A good way to monetize it is to offer basic information for free, then charge either a monthly membership, or a per-item charge for premium content. The premium content can include videos, e-books, or even sneak previews of content. As a bonus, you may attract more people to your website as the paywall gives people a sense of "exclusivity," making what you are offering more desirable.

Conclusion

Thank you again for downloading this book!

I hope this book was able to help you to discover new options to create passive income streams while you and your family live the life you have only imagined.

The next step is to try one, or several, techniques to earn cash instead of trading hours out of your life working for others.

Finally, if you enjoyed this book, please take the time to share your thoughts and post a review on Amazon. It would be greatly appreciated!

Thank you and good luck!

References

What is Passive Income: http://www.smartpassiveincome.com/passive-income-101/

A Beginners Guide For Starting An Amazon FBA Business: http://thesellingfamily.com/beginners-guide-starting-amazon-fba-business/

Smart Affiliate Marketing Strategies: http://www.smartpassiveincome.com/affiliate-marketing-strategies/

7 Big Mistakes New Affiliate Marketers Make: http://marketingland.com/7-big-mistakes-new-affiliate-marketers-make-19195

This Is How I Get Paid To Travel The World: http://expertvagabond.com/paid-to-travel-world/

How To Start A Travel Blog: A Step By Step Guide: http://expertvagabond.com/how-to-start-travel-blog/

11 Secrets To Becoming A Professional Travel Blogger: http://expertvagabond.com/professional-travel-blogger/

Why Travel Blogging is a Lousy Way to Earn Money Online: http://jetsetcitizen.com/cheap-travel/travel-blog-earn-money-online/

Guide to Dropshipping: https://www.shopify.com/guides/dropshipping

REITs: http://www.investopedia.com/articles/pf/06/realestateinvest.asp

www.ingramcontent.com/pod-product-compliance
Lightning Source LLC
Chambersburg PA
CBHW070227210526
45169CB00023B/1195